K M A Ahamed Zubair

Arwi or Arabu-Tamil in the Digital Age

K M A Ahamed Zubair

Arwi or Arabu-Tamil in the Digital Age

Challenges for Arwi or Arabu-Tamil Fonts in the twenty-first century

Noor Publishing

Imprint
Any brand names and product names mentioned in this book are subject to trademark, brand or patent protection and are trademarks or registered trademarks of their respective holders. The use of brand names, product names, common names, trade names, product descriptions etc. even without a particular marking in this work is in no way to be construed to mean that such names may be regarded as unrestricted in respect of trademark and brand protection legislation and could thus be used by anyone.

Cover image: www.ingimage.com

Publisher:
Noor Publishing
is a trademark of
Dodo Books Indian Ocean Ltd. and OmniScriptum S.R.L publishing group

120 High Road, East Finchley, London, N2 9ED, United Kingdom
Str. Armeneasca 28/1, office 1, Chisinau MD-2012, Republic of Moldova, Europe
Printed at: see last page
ISBN: 978-620-7-47872-9

Arwi or Arabu-Tamil in the Digital Age

Challenges for Arwi or Arabu-Tamil Fonts in the twenty-first century.

Dr.K.M.A.Ahamed Zubair

Associate Professor of Arabic, The New College,

Chennai 600 014, India

اللغة العربية تحمل كلمة الله، وروح محمد ﷺ، وسر الإسلام،

This work has been dedicated to the Indian Islamic
Missionaries (1500-1800)

Preface

In the history of Tamil Nadu and Sri Lanka, Arab Muslim traders and native Tamil converts to Islam interacted closely due to their trade activities. Although they shared a common religion, they spoke different languages. This led to a need for a bridge language, resulting in the development of Arwi-a form of Tamil written in an adapted Arabic script. Arwi, used from the eighth to the nineteenth century, was popular among Tamil-speaking Muslims. It facilitated the exchange of valuable ideas between Arab and Tamil cultures. However, by the twentieth century, Arwi began to decline, with no efforts made to preserve it. This book analyzes the Computational Study of Arwi Language, focusing on its Encoding Challenges and Solutions, particularly in the context of Unicode.

Dr K M A Ahamed Zubair

Contents

Arwi or Arabu-Tamil in the Digital Age

1.0 Introduction

Arwi, a unique language, was extensively used by Muslims in Tamil Nadu, India, and Sri Lanka. It emerged as a means of communication between settled Arab communities in Tamil Nadu and the local Tamil-speaking population, resulting from cultural interactions between seafaring Arabs and Tamil Muslims. Arwi gained popularity in Tamil Nadu and Ceylon (now Sri Lanka), boasting a rich literary tradition that has been partially preserved. Historical records indicate its use in far-eastern regions like Indonesia and Thailand.

Arwi played a crucial role in transforming the daily lives of Muslim Tamil societies in Tamil Nadu and Sri Lanka, facilitating the writing of religious, literary, and poetic texts. The script of Arwi, representing Tamil (a left-to-right script), adopts an Arabic-style format (right-to-left script). This unique script was widely adopted by Asian Muslim Tamils for everyday communication. From the eighth to the nineteenth century, Arwi flourished among Tamil-speaking Muslims in Tamil Nadu and Ceylon, retaining popularity among Ceylonese Muslims to this day, who hold its literature in high regard.

There are significant socio-religious similarities between the Muslims of South India and Sri Lanka, summarized as follows (Maharoof, 409):

a. Both Sri Lankan Muslims and those in Tamil Nadu primarily speak Tamil.

b. The Tamil spoken by Muslim communities in Sri Lanka and Tamil Nadu incorporates a substantial number of Turko-Perso-Arabic loanwords.

c. Close cultural ties exist between Muslims in Sri Lanka and Tamil Nadu.

d. Over the ages, Muslim missionaries from Tamil Nadu have influenced religious beliefs in Sri Lanka, contributing to the establishment of Tariqa. Many Qadiriyyah sub-fraternities in Sri Lanka trace their origins to centers in Kilakarai, Kayalpattanam, and Kottaru, located in Ramnad, Tirunelveli districts, and Tamil Nadu near the Kerala border.

2.0 Origin of Arwi

Arwi emerged among Arabs who settled in Tamil Nadu, where they learned Tamil using the Arabic script to write in Tamil. Its origins trace back to the earliest contacts between Arabs and Tamil Nadu (Rahman, P. 23). The Muslim communities of Sarandib (Sri Lanka) and Tamil Nadu used Arwi effectively to preserve their cultural identity without compromising their religious beliefs (Shuaib, 91). Arwi signifies a cultural blend between Arabs and Tamil-speaking Muslims, combining Arabic and Tamil while employing Arabic script.

With the rise of Islam, settled Arabs in the region naturally became representatives of the religion. Over time, local conversions to Islam occurred, leading to closer interactions between communities sharing a religion but speaking different languages due to commercial ties. This culminated in the creation of Arwi as a link-language. Arwi represents a fusion of two significant languages - Semitic-Arabic and Dravidian-Tamil.

The Arabs of Tamil Nadu, recognizing Tamil's antiquity akin to Arabic, learned it using their Arabic script and began expressing ideas in this hybrid language. Initially,

Arabs adopted a colloquial style, ignoring Tamil grammar similar to later English use. Before writing Tamil in Arabic script, Arabs primarily relied on oral recollection of daily words, later transcribed into Arabic script, marking the birth of Arwi (Samuel, 273). Initially, Arab expressions were absorbed by Tamilians, becoming crucial in commercial settings and remaining in use today not only among Tamilians but also across India.

Certain Islamic terms like Rasul (Messenger), Sahabah (Companions of the Prophet), Wajib (Obligatory), Jannath (Paradise), Jahannam (Hell), Iman (Belief), Taqwa (Piety) lack clear equivalents in Tamil. Hence, Arwi words are preferred for better expression and comprehension by Tamil Muslims. Arwi retains the essence of spoken Tamil, adorned with the beauty of the Arabic script through the adaptation of Arabic letters with diacritical marks. Despite now existing informally, Arwi continues to be a part of traditional Indian Tamil Muslim and Sri Lankan Moor families' spoken language, enriching their daily conversations (e.g., *Museebah* for calamity, *Mowth* for death, *Janazah* for funeral, *Raahat* for relief, *Shifaa* for healing, *Khair* for goodness, *Wallahi* for by God's name).

3.0 Place of Origin

Arwi's prevalence in Colombo, Kayalpattinam, and Kilakarai suggests usage dating back to the eighth century CE (Samuel, 275), showcasing joint efforts by Arabs and Tamil Muslims in its formation. Originating along the South-West Coast of Ceylon and the South-East Coast of India, particularly in Kayalpattinam, Arwi was enriched, promoted, and developed, serving as a catalyst for the advancement of Arab and Tamil cultures.

4.0 Tamil, Arabic, and Arwi Scripts

Arwi / ArabuTamil Alphabets					
چ	ج	ث	ت	ب	ا
ذ	دٜ	ڊ	د	خ	ح
ص	ش	س	ز	رٜ	ر
ع	ظ	ط	صٜ	ضٜ	ض
ك	ق	ف	ف	غ	ڮ
ن	ن	ن	م	ل	كٜ
		ي	لاء	ه	و

Arabic script operates on a consonantal system, featuring distinct symbols or letters solely for consonants, with vowels as optional and represented by diacritical marks. Arabic comprises 28 consonants and is typically written from right to left.

Tamil, on the other hand, consists of 30 basic letters, including 12 vowels and 18 consonants, following a syllabic writing system where combinations of consonants and vowels are represented by syllabic symbols. Tamil employs 216 syllabic symbols alongside its basic vowels and consonants, written from left to right.

The Arwi script uniquely represents the Tamil language using an Arabic-style script. In addition to Arabic script, 12 characters were incorporated, facilitating the inclusion of vowels. For vowels shared with Arabic (-a-, -i-, -u-, -aa-, -ii-, -uu-) and diphthongs (-ai- and -au-), the same diacritical signs used in Arabic (fatha, qasra, damma) are employed for short vowels, with long vowels indicated by additional alif, yaa, and waaw, respectively. Furthermore, new characters were introduced to represent Tamil sounds absent in Arabic.

Arwi comprises 40 letters, with 28 derived from Arabic and 12 devised by adding marks and dots to the original Arabic alphabet. Notably, 18 Arabic letters lack phonetic equivalents in Tamil, while ten Tamil letters and two vowel sounds have no equivalents in Arabic.

In summary, the Arwi alphabet is essentially the Arabic alphabet augmented with 12 additional letters to accommodate Tamil vowels and certain Tamil consonants that differ from Arabic phonetics. Arwi incorporates 7 letters that align with English phonetics.

5.0 Formation and Construction of Arwi Letters and Vowel Marks from Arabic Alphabet

The formation and construction of eleven Arwi letters and two vowel marks from the existing Arabic alphabet are detailed as follows (Zubair, 2014, 60-62):

1. Adding two dots to an existing dot above a letter "ج",results in the Tamil sound "ச" (pronounced like the 'ch' in 'much').
2. Adding a dot below a letter "د", creates the equivalent of Tamil "ட" (similar to 'd' in "burden" in English.
3. Placing two dots below a letter "د", produces the sound of Tamil "ட" (equivalent to 'tt' in English).
4. A dot placed below an Arabic letter "ر", used for Tamil

"ற" (akin to 'r' in English).

5. Adding a dot below "ض" creates the sound in Tamil resembling "ழ", which has no direct English equivalent but is similar to the sound of 'zh' when written together.

6. Adding a dot below "ص" creates the sound in Tamil resembling "ள", which has no direct English equivalent .

7. Adding three dots below the Arabic letter "ع" yields the sound similar to Tamil "ங", (pronounced as the 'ng' in 'Going').

8. Adding a dot below "ف", a softened Tamil letter "ப" creates the equivalent of "ப" (similar to 'p' in English), indicating that Arwi's evolution was distinct from Persian influences.

9. Placing a dot below "ک " produces the sound akin to Tamil "க" (similar to 'g' in English).

10. Placing a dot below the Tamil letter "ண" results in the letter "ن", which also lacks an English equivalent.

11. Adding two dots below a letter "ن", in the Arabic alphabet , representing a sound similar to Tamil "ஞ" (pronounced like 'gn' in English, as in 'sign').

12. To produce the vowel sound "o" (as in 'wonder'), the "Ko Pesh" sign is placed on top of any letter.

13. Placing the same sign under a letter creates the

vowel sound "e" (as in 'men'), known as "Ko Zayr".

These transformations demonstrate how Arwi adapted the Arabic script to incorporate Tamil sounds and vowels, showcasing a unique synthesis of linguistic elements from both languages.

6.0 Handwritten Specimen of Arwi Writing

(Transliteration of the above Invitation in Tamil)

சோனக இஸ்லாமிய கலாச்சார நிலையம் (அமைக்கப்பட்டது)

தங்களுக்கு எமது நல்வாழ்த்தும் சோபனமும் கூறுவதோடு கொழும்பு கோட்டை பிரிஸ்டல் வீதி, 27 ஆம் நம்பர் இல்லமாகிய இஸ்லாமிய கலாச்சார நிலைய புதுக்கட்டிட திறப்பு விழாவிற்கு 1965, மே மாதம் 30 ஆம் தேதி, ஹிஜ்ரா 1385 முஹர்ரம் 28 பிறை ஞாயிறு பிற்பகல் 4:15 மணிக்கு சங்கமிக்குமாறு தங்களை அன்புடன் அழைக்கிறோம்.

கௌரவ பிரதமர் திரு.டட்லி சேனாநாயக அவர்கள் ஞாபகார்த்த பலகையை திரை நீக்கம் செய்வார்கள். தலைமை நிலையத் தலைவர் ஜனாப் சர் ராஜிக் ஃபரீத் அவர்கள் புதுக்கட்டிடத்தை திறந்து வைப்பார்கள்.

(Translation of the above Invitation in English)

Sonaga Islamic Cultural Centre (Established)

We send you our felicitations, greetings, and cordially invite you to attend the opening ceremony of our new building at No. 27 Bristol Street, Fort, Colombo, on the 30th May 1965, the 28th Day of Muharram 1385, Sunday afternoon, 4:15 pm.

Honourable Prime Minister Mr. Dudley Senanayake will unveil the commemoration block. The President of the centre, Sir Razik Fareed will open the building.

8.0 Computer-Encoded Specimen of Arwi Writing

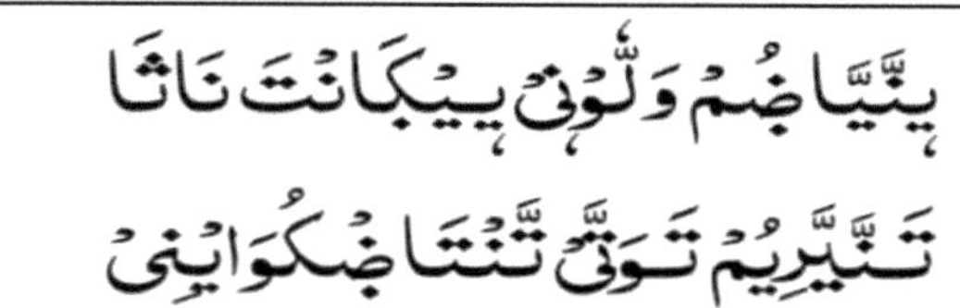

The following are a few couplets from an Arwi poem written by Syed Mohammed Imam al-Aroos (1816-1898 A.D.):

(Transliteration of the above couplet in Tamil)

என்னை ஆளும் வல்லோனே ஏகாந்த நாதா
தன்னை அறியும் தவத்தை தந்தாள்குவாய் நீ

(Translation of the above couplet in English)

O Almighty Who rules over me! O my Master who is the

only Lord! Bless me with the boon of realizing the insignificance of myself.

(Transliteration of the above couplet in Tamil)

أُنَّيَّلَاثُ وِيْرُيَارَىْ وِضِغْـِيْنْ
يِنَّىْ وِدُّمْحَقَّاكَ أُنِّلْ أُضِغِْيْنْ

உன்னை அல்லாது வேறு யாரை விளிப்பேன்
என்னை விட்டும் ஹக்காக உன்னில் ஒளிப்பேன்

(Translation of the above couplet in English)

Whom can I beseech except Thee! I will [leave my wretched self and] annihilate in Thee!

7.0 Manuscript Form Specimen of Arwi Writing

بسم الله الرحمن الرحيم

These specimens demonstrate the unique script and language style of Arwi, showcasing its blend of Tamil and Arabic elements in both handwritten and computer-encoded formats.

8.0 Specimen of Arwi Appreciation Certificate for Participation/Presentation in a Competition

The following certificate is issued to participants by the "Mad'harul Faizeen Society" in Kayalpattinam, recognizing their involvement in an online presentation or speech contest, offered by the society:

மத்ஹர் அல்ஃபாயிஜின் சங்கம்

பாராட்டுச் சான்றிதழ்

இந்த பாராட்டுச் சான்றிதழ் அவர்களுக்கு இணைய வழி கிராஅத் / பேச்சு போட்டியில் பங்கேற்றதை பாராட்டும் விதமாக காயல்பட்டணம் மத்ஹர் அல் - ஃபாயிஜின் சங்கத்தால் வழங்கப்படுகிறது

உதவி மேலாளர் (கையொப்பம்)

செயலாளர் (கையொப்பம்)

Translation:

Mad'harul Faizeen Society

Certificate of Appreciation

This certificate is presented to the participants for their involvement in an online presentation or speech contest, organized by the Mad'harul Faizeen Society in Kayalpattinam.

Supervisor (Signature)

Coordinator (Signature)

9.0 Status and Recognition of Arwi

The United Nations has recognized Arwi as one of the approved languages globally. An article on the life of the Prophet, authored by Mohammed Yasinn, was published in "The UNESCO COURIER" by UNESCO in August-September 1981 (Shuaib, 90).

10.0 Development of Arwi Language and Literature

Arwi emerged as the primary language of the Muslim community, serving as a medium for their daily affairs, including business transactions, property dealings, correspondence, and social interactions.

The literature in Arwi, comprising prose and poetry, covers a diverse range of subjects, including architecture, astronomy, biography, Quranic commentary, elegy, fiction, history, horticulture, medicine, moral science, sexology, sports, creed, dictionary, Islamic jurisprudence, logic, satire, mysticism, among others.

This language flourished during the early medieval ages, with a predominant focus on religious literature. Tamil scholars significantly contributed to the language and literature development of Arwi, producing Quran translations and other religious texts.

The literary origin of Arwi can be traced to Kayalpattnam, Melapalayam, and other prominent Labbai towns in the Tirunelveli District (Samuel, P. 271). The orthographic practices varied among Arwi authors, demonstrating diverse linguistic forms and vocabularies within the language. Arwi's structure and development principles are akin to other Islamic speech and writing systems, such as Swahili in Tanzania, Jaawi in Malaysia, and languages in Turkey, Uzbekistan, Berber, Somalia, and Malay.

Approximately four hundred years ago, Hafiz Amir Wali Appa, a saint from Kayalpattinam, introduced a new literary style to Arwi writing, revitalizing the language after Portuguese colonization around 1600 (Zubair, 2006, 189). Hafiz Amir Wali Appa's literary contributions elevated Arwi's status, with his tomb located on Weaver's Street in Kayalpattinam.

11.0 Contribution of Arwi

The voluminous literature produced in Arwi by Muslim scholars played a crucial role in the religious revival of the Muslim community after the cultural devastation caused by Portuguese colonization in the sixteenth century (1528 and 1537). This literature covered a wide array of subjects including jurisprudence, Sufism, law, medicine, and poetry, serving as a bridge language for Tamil Muslims to learn Arabic.

Arwi compositions, including devotional songs used in Islamic ceremonies, were originally written in Arwi by their authors. For instance, "Thalai Fathiha," a well-known Arwi song, is devoutly sung by women during ceremonies.

There exist thousands of Arwi books covering diverse subjects, systematically organized in the Madras Archives Catalogues since 1890. These catalogues cover various periods including 1890-1901, 1901-1910, 1911-1915, and 1921-25. According to these catalogues, there are more than 3,000 Arwi books documented.

One of the most significant contributions is the Arwi Dictionary spanning four substantial volumes authored by

Hakkim Muhammed Abdullah Sahib. This literature not only enriched the knowledge of Tamil Muslims about their religion and culture but also facilitated a better understanding of Arabic literature (Samuel, 277).

Encoding Arwi language using Unicode presents several challenges from a computational perspective, particularly in terms of typing and printing Arwi characters on computers. The Unicode standard, developed by the Unicode Consortium, aims to create a universal character set that supports all writing systems and symbols in common use globally.

Here are some key points regarding encoding Arwi language with Unicode:

1. Universal Standard: Unicode aims to cover all writing systems and symbols, including characters used in Arwi, within a single character set.
2. Efficient Encoding: Unicode uses an efficient encoding scheme that avoids complexities like code page switching or special states, ensuring straightforward representation of characters.
3. Uniform Encoding Width: Each character in Unicode is encoded as a 16-bit value (or sometimes more), ensuring a consistent representation across different

scripts.

4. Unambiguous Encoding: Unicode ensures that each character is uniquely represented by a specific 16-bit value, providing clarity and consistency in character encoding.

For Arwi language, which is a blend of Arabic and Tamil scripts, Unicode provides a range of characters that can be used for typing and encoding Arwi text. The Arabic Unicode range (U+0600 to U+06FF) and additional characters from other ranges (such as Syriac) can be leveraged to represent the entire Arwi script.

However, despite the availability of Unicode characters, there are challenges related to practical implementation:

- Typing Challenges: Users may face difficulty in inputting Arwi characters directly, especially if keyboard layouts do not support these characters.
- Printing Issues: Arwi script may encounter problems during printing, particularly if the fonts or rendering systems are not optimized for Unicode representation.
- Font Support: While Unicode provides the character codes, the availability of fonts that support Arwi characters may be limited, affecting both display and

printing.

To address these challenges, efforts are needed to ensure widespread adoption of Unicode for Arwi script, including the development of compatible keyboard layouts, font support, and improvements in printing technologies to fully realize the benefits of standardized character encoding.

12.0 Challenges of encoding Arwi script using Unicode and suggesting substitute characters for Arwi letters

The suggested Unicode substitutions are as follows:

Arwi / ArabuTamil Alphabets					
ا	ب	ت	ث	ج	چ
ح	خ	د	د	ي	ذ
ر	ڔ	ز	س	ش	ص
ض	ض	صٜ	ط	ظ	ع
چ	غ	ف	ف	ق	ك
كٜ	ل	م	ن	ن	ن
و	ه	لاء	ي		

1. Arwi Letters with No Arabic Equivalents and Their Substitutions:
   - Arwi Character: ஞ (Equivalent to Tamil letter "ஞ")
   - Substitution: Arabic letter Saad with two dots below (U+069D)
   - Arwi Character: க (Equivalent to Tamil letter "க")
   - Substitution: Arabic letter Ayn with three dots above (U+06A0)
   - Arwi Character: 6T (Specific Arwi character)
   - Substitution: Arabic letter kaaf with dot above (U+06AC)
   - Arwi Character: ய (Equivalent to Tamil letter "ய")
   - Substitution: Arabic Empty Centre Low Stop (U+06EA)
2. Encoding Remarks:
   - suggested Arabic Unicode characters as substitutions for these Arwi characters, which don't have direct counterparts in the Arabic script.
3. Unicode Encoding for Arwi Script:
   - Ensure that the Arwi script is encoded using the appropriate Arabic Unicode characters as suggested substitutions for the non-equivalent

Arwi letters.

4. Availability of Unicode Characters:

    ○ Some Arwi characters may require creative substitutions due to the limitations of the Unicode character set. Using similar Arabic characters with specific diacritics or modifiers can be a practical approach.

In summary, encoding Arwi script in Unicode involves using available Arabic characters and applying necessary diacritics or modifiers to represent the unique sounds and letters of the Arwi language. The suggested substitutions provide a workaround for characters not directly supported by the Unicode standard. This approach helps maintain consistency and accessibility for Arwi script in digital environments.

Based on the above descriptions, here's a summary of the Arwi letters and their corresponding Unicode characters as mentioned:

- ڄ

    ○ Arwi Equivalent: This letter is used in Persian and Urdu languages.
    ○ Unicode Character: Arabic letter Haa with two dots above (U+06C1)

- خ
    - Arwi Equivalent: This is an Arwi letter available in Unicode, also used in Persian and Urdu languages.
    - Unicode Character: Arabic letter Khaa (U+062E)
- د
    - Arwi Equivalent: This is an Arabic letter available in Unicode.
    - Unicode Character: Arabic letter Daal (U+062F)
- س
    - Arwi Equivalent: This is an Arabic letter available in Unicode.
    - Unicode Character: Arabic letter Seen (U+0633)
- An Arwi Alphabet. Available in Unicode. Used in Sindhi and Early Persian languages also.
    - Unicode Character: Specific Arwi letter available in Unicode, used in Sindhi and Early Persian languages.
- An Arwi Alphabet. Available in Unicode. Used in Sindhi language also.
    - Unicode Character: Specific Arwi letter available in Unicode, used in Sindhi language.
- An Arabic Alphabet. Available in Unicode.
    - Unicode Character: Arabic letter Seen (U+0633) or another Arabic letter depending on context.

- An Arabic Alphabet. Available in Unicode.
    - Unicode Character: Arabic letter (specific character) available in Unicode.
- An Arabic Alphabet. Available in Unicode.
    - Unicode Character: Arabic letter (specific character) available in Unicode.
- An Arwi Alphabet. Available in Unicode. Used in Sindhi and Early Persian languages also.
- Unicode Character: Specific Arwi letter available in Unicode, used in Sindhi and Early Persian languages.
- An Arabic Alphabet. Available in Unicode.
- Unicode Character: Arabic letter (specific character) available in Unicode.
- An Arabic Alphabet. Available in Unicode.
- Unicode Character: Arabic letter (specific character) available in Unicode.

- An Arabic Alphabet. Available in Unicode.
    - Unicode Character: Arabic letter (specific character) available in Unicode.
- ش
    - Arwi Equivalent: This is an Arabic letter available in Unicode.
    - Unicode Character: Arabic letter Sheen (U+0634)

- An Arabic Alphabet. Available in Unicode.
    - Unicode Character: Arabic letter (specific character) available in Unicode.
- An Arabic Alphabet. Available in Unicode.
    - Unicode Character: Arabic letter (specific character) available in Unicode.
- An Arwi Alphabet. Available in Unicode. It is an Extended Arabic letter.
    - Unicode Character: Specific Arwi letter available in Unicode, possibly an extended Arabic letter.
- ص
    - Arwi Equivalent: This Arwi letter can be represented by the Arabic letter Saad with two dots below, used also in the Turkish language.
    - Unicode Character: Arabic letter Saad with two dots below (U+069D)
- An Arabic Alphabet. Available in Unicode.
    - Unicode Character: Arabic letter (specific character) available in Unicode.
- An Arabic Alphabet. Available in Unicode.
    - Unicode Character: Arabic letter (specific character) available in Unicode.
- An Arabic Alphabet. Available in Unicode.
    - Unicode Character: Arabic letter (specific character) available in Unicode.

- An Arwi Alphabet. Available in Unicode. Instead of the Arabic letter Ayn with three dots below, we can employ the Arabic letter Ayn with three dots above. Used in old Malay language also.
  - Unicode Character: Arabic letter Ayn with three dots above (U+06A0)

These Unicode characters enable the representation of Arwi script accurately, even for letters that do not have direct equivalents in standard Arabic. The use of existing Unicode characters ensures compatibility and proper rendering in digital environments.

Here is the continuation of the Arwi letters and their corresponding Unicode characters based on the provided descriptions:

- غ
  - Arwi Equivalent: This Arwi letter corresponds to the Arabic letter Ghain.
  - Unicode Character: Arabic letter Ghain (U+063A)
- An Arabic Alphabet. Available in Unicode.
  - Unicode Character: Arabic letter (specific character) available in Unicode.
- An Arwi Alphabet. Available in Unicode. Used in Ingush language spoken in Ingushetia and

Uzbekistan

- Unicode Character: Specific Arwi letter used in the Ingush language, likely represented in Unicode.

- An Arabic Alphabet. Available in Unicode.
  - Unicode Character: Arabic letter (specific character) available in Unicode.

- ڬ

  - Arwi Equivalent: This Arwi letter corresponds to the Arabic letter Kaf.
  - Unicode Character: Arabic letter Kaf (U+0643)

- An Arwi Alphabet. Available in Unicode. Instead of the Arabic letter Kaaf with one dot below, we can employ the Arabic letter Kaaf with one dot above. Used in old Malay language also.
  - Unicode Character: Arabic letter Kaaf with one dot above (U+06AC)

- An Arabic Alphabet. Available in Unicode.
  - Unicode Character: Arabic letter (specific character) available in Unicode.

- An Arabic Alphabet. Available in Unicode.
  - Unicode Character: Arabic letter (specific character) available in Unicode.

- An Arabic Alphabet. Available in Unicode.
  - Unicode Character: Arabic letter (specific

character) available in Unicode.

- An Arwi Alphabet. Available in Unicode. Extended Arabic letter also.
  - Unicode Character: Specific Arwi letter, possibly an extended Arabic letter, available in Unicode.
- An Arwi Alphabet. Available in Unicode. Developed exclusively for Arwi language.
  - Unicode Character: Specific Arwi letter developed exclusively for the Arwi language, represented in Unicode.

These Unicode characters provide the necessary encoding for representing Arwi script accurately, including letters that are unique to the Arwi language and may not have direct equivalents in standard Arabic. Utilizing Unicode ensures compatibility and proper rendering of Arwi text in digital environments.

Here is the completion of the list of Arwi letters and symbols along with their corresponding Unicode characters:

- An Arabic Alphabet. Available in Unicode.
  - Unicode Character: Arabic letter (specific character) available in Unicode.
- An Arabic Alphabet. Available in Unicode.

- ○ Unicode Character: Arabic letter (specific character) available in Unicode.

- ه
  - ○ Arwi Equivalent: This Arwi letter corresponds to the Arabic letter Ha.
  - ○ Unicode Character: Arabic letter Ha (U+0647)

- S_ص
  - ○ Unicode Character: Specific Arwi letter or symbol represented by the character 'S' in Unicode.

- An Arabic Alphabet. Available in Unicode.
  - ○ Unicode Character: Arabic letter (specific character) available in Unicode.

- /An Arwi Vowel. Available in Unicode. Instead of the Vowel sign (the symbol like of Apostrophe) placed below the Consonant, we can employ an Arabic Empty Centre Low Stop symbol. Used as a Quranic Annotation Sign also.
  - ○ Unicode Character: Arabic Empty Centre Low Stop symbol (U+06EA)

- An Arwi Vowel. Available in Unicode. It is a Symbol of Arabic inverted Dammah called Ko Pesh or Ulta Pesh. Used in Kashmiri and Urdu Languages also.
  - ○ Unicode Character: Symbol representing Arabic inverted Dammah (U+0656)

These Unicode characters, including specific Arabic and Arwi letters, vowels, and symbols, enable proper representation and encoding of Arwi script for digital applications and text processing. The availability of these characters in Unicode ensures compatibility and correct rendering across different devices and platforms.

It's clear that Arwi, once a vibrant language with deep cultural and religious significance for the Tamil Muslim community, has unfortunately experienced a decline in recent centuries. Several factors have contributed to this decline, including the lack of modern printing facilities, the adoption of Urdu as a dominant Islamic curriculum, and the exclusion of Arwi from formal education systems.

Conclusion

To revitalize and preserve Arwi language and literature, the following steps are suggested:

a. Preservation and Publication: Efforts should be made to collect existing Arwi language books and manuscripts, and to re-print and publish them for wider access and preservation.

b. Inclusion in Madrasah Curriculum: Arwi language should be reintroduced and made compulsory in all Madrasahs (Islamic schools) across Tamil Nadu and Sri Lanka to ensure its transmission to future generations.

c. Integration into School Curriculum: Arwi language and literature should be included as part of the school curriculum in mainstream educational institutions to promote wider awareness and appreciation.

d. Community Engagement: Encourage the Tamil Muslim community to actively use Arwi in their daily lives, including religious practices, social interactions, and cultural events.

e. Publication of Periodicals: Reintroduce periodicals and magazines in Arwi language to foster a culture of reading and writing in the language.

By implementing these measures, there's hope for a revival and renaissance of Arwi language and literature, ensuring its cultural and historical significance is preserved and celebrated for generations to come.

It's evident that the decline of Arwi language and literature stems from various challenges, including the lack of modern printing facilities and the adoption of Urdu as a dominant Islamic curriculum in the early 20th century, which did not prioritize Arwi's unique cultural and historical roots in southern South Asia.

To address the issues and challenges faced in encoding and printing Arwi texts, adopting Unicode characters can offer a practical solution. Unicode provides a standardized and universally recognized set of characters that can facilitate the typing, encoding, and printing of Arwi language books. By leveraging Unicode, the process of publishing Arwi literature can become more accessible and efficient.

There is a wealth of unpublished Arwi literary works in handwritten or manuscript form, numbering over 4,000 books. Efforts to publish these works are essential to preserve and promote Arwi language and literature. Open source initiatives like Wikipedia can serve as platforms to share these literary treasures with a global audience, contributing to the preservation and appreciation of Arwi heritage.

By addressing the challenges in printing and encoding, and by promoting the publication and accessibility of Arwi literature, there is hope for a revival and renewed interest in this culturally rich language for future generations.

References

Abdullah , Farhanah, and Rahman, Asyraf Hj Ab.2017. Contributions of Jawi Script and Jawi Writings to Islamic Discourse.Kuala Lumpur:INSPIRE Universiti Sultan Zainal Abidin UniSZA.

Abdullah,Taufik.1991.Zakat Collection and Distribution in Indonesia.In The Islamic Voluntary Sector in Southeast Asia:Islamic and EconomicDevelopment of Southeast Asia,ed.Mohamed Ariff. Singapore:Institute of Southeast Asian Studies.

Agoncillo, Teodoro. 1990. History of the Filipino People. Manila: R.P. Garcia Publishing Co.

Al-Attas, Syed Muhammad Naquib.1993.Islam and Secularism. Kuala Lumpur: International Institute of Islamic Thought and Civilization.

Al-Ghazālī, Imām Abdul Ḥāmid.1982. Imām Al-Ghazālī's Iḥyā''UlūmAl-Dīn. ed.Maulana Faslul Karim.New Delhi:Nusrat Ali Nasri for Kitab Bhavan.

Ariff, Mohamed,ed.1991.The Islamic Voluntary Sector in Southeast Asia: Islamic and Economic Development of SoutheastAsia.Singapore:Institute of Southeast Asian Studies.

Gamon, Alizaman Dumangcag.2014. Societal Transformation and the Muslims in the Philippines: Islamic Legal and Educational Institutions since1970s. Ph.D.diss. International Institute of Islamic Thought and Civilization.

Hassan,M.Kamal.2011.Voice of Islamic Moderation from the Malay World.Ipoh, Perak:Emeging Markets Innovative Research (M) Sdn.Bhd.

Ibrahim, Norhasnira.2015.Jawi Script in Hadith Literatures in Malaysia: Issues and Challenges.IPEDR 83:94-98.

Johns A H.1996."In the Language of the Divine: The Contribution of Arabic." In Illuminations: The Writing Traditions of Indonesia, eds.Kumar,Ann. and McGlynn, John H. Jakarta: Lontar, , 33-48.

Kokan, Mohammad Yousuf.1974. Arabic and Persian in Carnatic (1710-1960), Madras :Hafiza House.

Maharoof, M M M.1995."Spoken Tamil dialect of the

Muslims of Sri Lanka: Language as Identity classifier. Islamic Studies 34 (4):402-12

Mukti, and Jazadi,Iwan.2015.The Significance of Total Physical Response(TPR) Method In Teaching Jawi Alphabet To Young Generation.Journal Cendekia 15(July-September):198-210.

Rahim ,Abdur M R M. 1976. Islamia Kalai Kalanjiam[Islamic Tamil Encyclopedia].Madras:Universal Publishers.

Rahman ,Asyraf Hj Ab.and Ali, Abdul Manan .and Abdullah, Farhanah Bt.and Kadir, Firdaus Khairi Abdul. and Adam,Fadzli. and Ismail, Daud.2017.Methods of Learning and Writing Jawi Scripts within the Malay

Community: Past and Present Experiences. International Journal of Management and Applied Science 3(10):01-07.

Rahman, Abdur H. 1985 Origin and Development of Arabu-Tamil in Tamil Nadu. M.Phil. diss. University of Madras.

Rahman, Rizwanur.2006.al-Lisan al-Arwi[Arwi Dialect].Thaqafatul Hind 57(2):188-204.

Salleh .Siti Hawa Haji.2010. Malay Literature of the 19th Century.Malaysia:Institut Terjemahan Negara Malaysia

Berhad.

Samuel, John G. 2010. Tamil as a classical Language.Chennai: Institute of Asian Studies Press.

Sharom, Ahmat, and Sharom Siddique.1987.Muslim Society, Higher Education and Development in Southeast Asia. Singapore:ISEAS.

Shuyab, Tayka .1993. Arabic, Arwi and Persian in Sarandib and Tamil Nadu,Chennai: Imaamul Aroos Trust.

Silvey, Rachel.2005. "Transnational Islam: Indonesian Migrant Domestic Workers in Saudi Arabia." In Geographies of Muslim Women: Gender, Religion, and Space, eds. by Walid ,Ghazi and

Falah,Nagel.Caroline:Guilford Press, 133-54.

Zainab, A N.2001. Digitisation of an endangered written language: The case of the Jawi script. Presented at the International Symposium on Languages in Cyberspace, Seoul.

Zubair, Ahamed K M A. 2013. Arabu-Tamil: Its Alphabet, Ligatures, Phonetic Equivalents and Combining Procedures. JARJ-Jamals Academic Research Journal 7(July- December):104-119.

Zubair, Ahamed K M A. 2014. Arwi or Arabu-Tamil. Germany: Lambert Academic Publishing.

Zubair, Ahamed K M A. 2016. Phonetical, Philology and Orthographical Study Arabu-Tamil Language: Encoding Issues and Solutions with special reference to Unicode. NOVA Journal of Arabic Studies 7(2): 01-23

Zubair, Ahamed K M A. 2017. Al-Lugha al- Arwiyyah [Arwi Language]. Latvia: Noor Publishing.

Printed by Books on Demand GmbH, Norderstedt / Germany